It's RAGTIME!

8 Ragtime Solos and Arrangements for the Intermediate Pianist

W.T. Skye Garcia

For anyone who has experienced the music of ragtime, it is easy to see how pianists of all ages and abilities quickly develop a fascination for this spirited style of music. I began trying to teach myself to play Scott Joplin's *Maple Leaf Rag* sometime during my first six months of piano lessons—without my teacher's knowledge!

Chief among the characteristics of ragtime is a melody containing varying degrees of syncopation. This syncopated melody is in contrast to a steady pulse maintained by the accompaniment. As such, the study of ragtime can serve to further students' awareness of some of the more advanced rhythmic complexities that occur in music, as well as enhance their overall physical coordination at the piano.

It was not these teaching considerations, however, that led me to spend countless hours at my piano "hammering out" Joplin's rag, but rather the sheer joy of hearing ragtime come alive under my fingertips. This is the experience I hope each of you who plays these pieces can share.

W.T. Skye Garcia

Alfred

ISBN 0-7390-2789-1

Step Right Up!

The Ionian Rag*

W. T. Skye Garcia

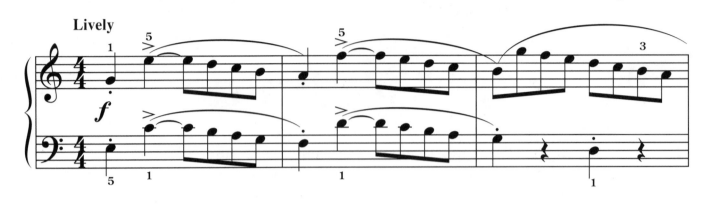

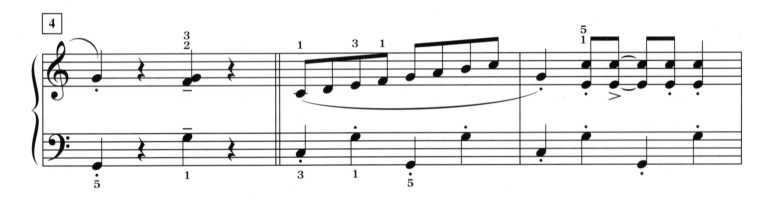

Ionian is a musical term that refers to the pattern of whole steps and half steps found in a major scale.

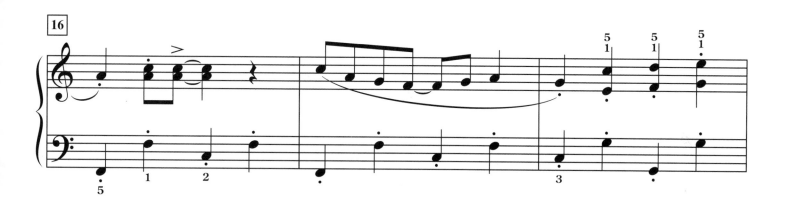

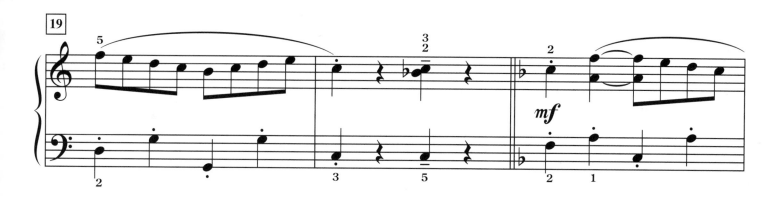

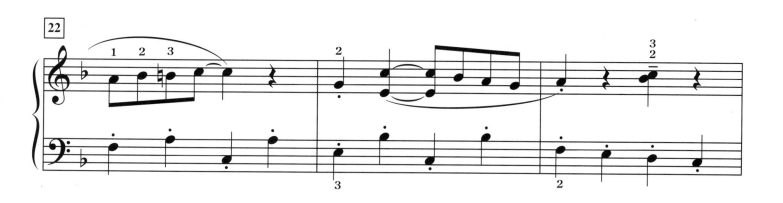

Waltzin' in Ragtime

W. T. Skye Garcia

Scalawag Rag

W. T. Skye Garcia

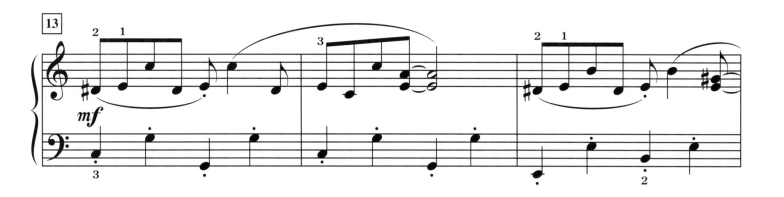

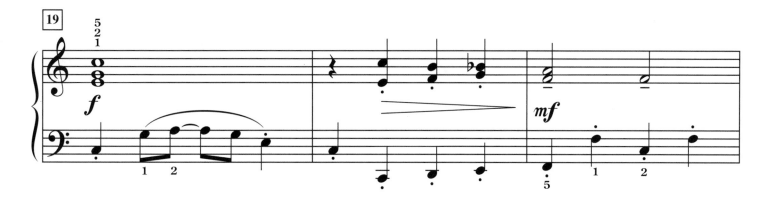

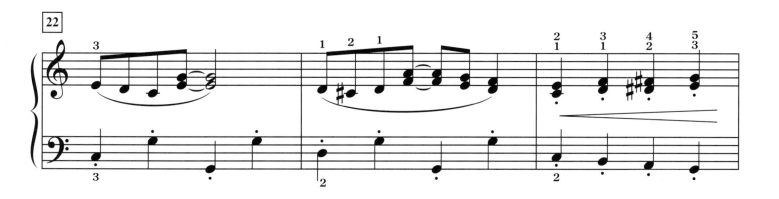

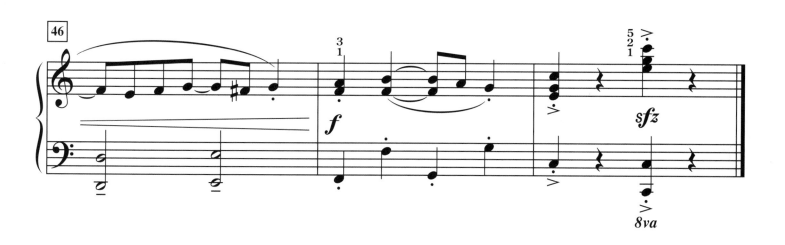

Ragtime Serenade

W. T. Skye Garcia

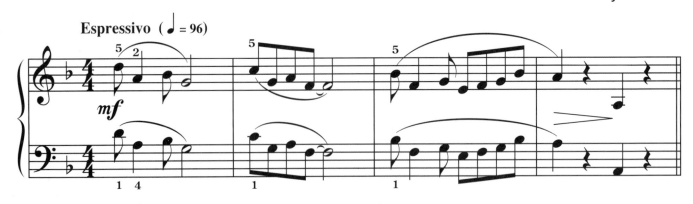

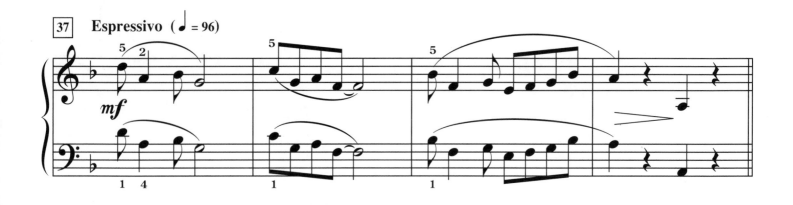

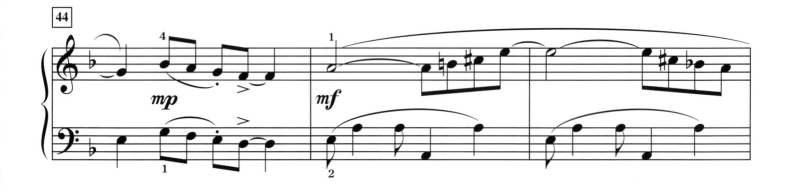

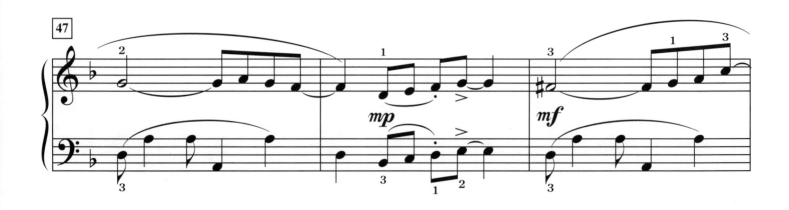

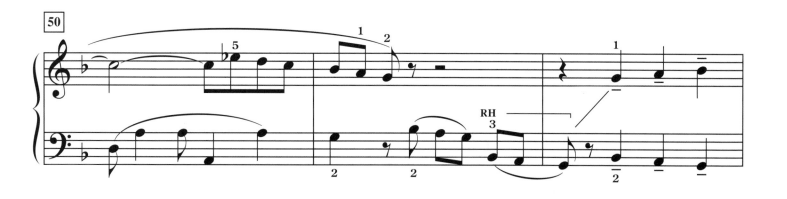

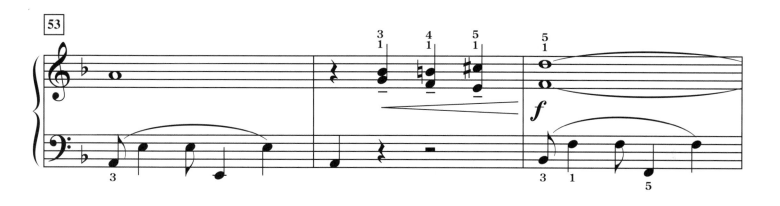

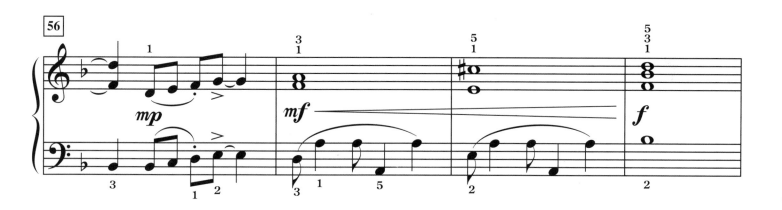

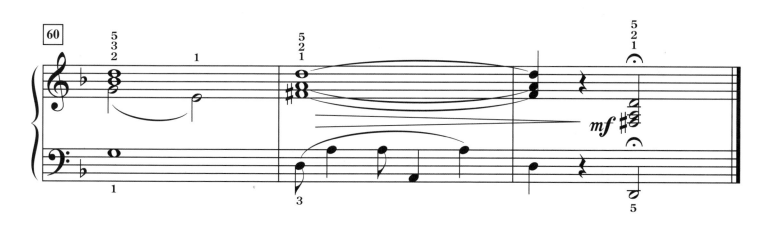

The Entertainer

Scott Joplin
Arr. by W. T. Skye Garcia

Not fast

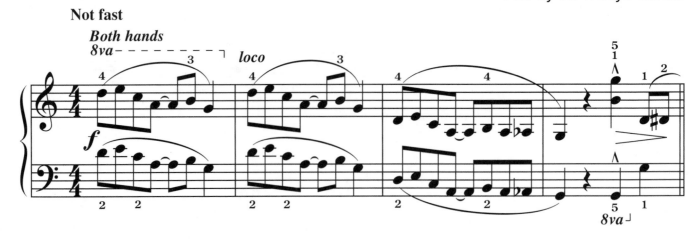

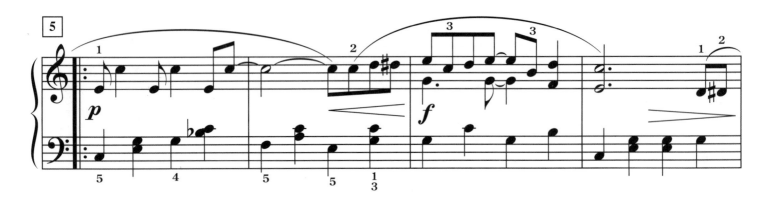

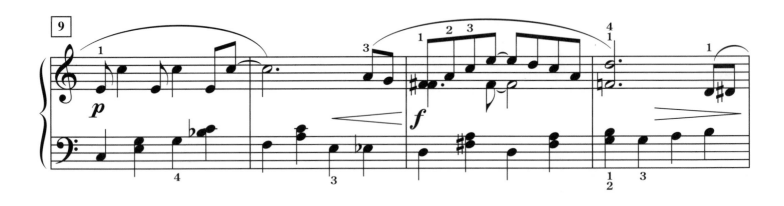

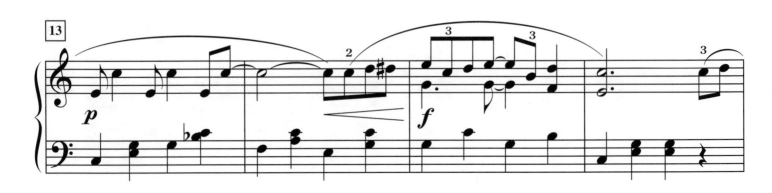

LH detached

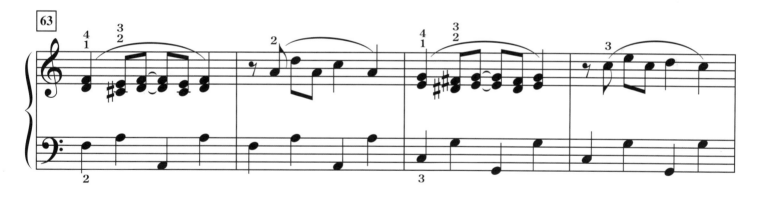

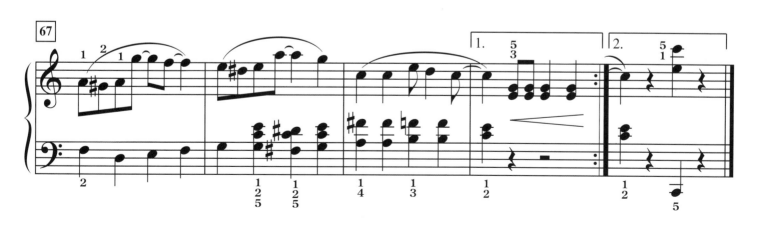

Maple Leaf Rag

Scott Joplin
Arr. by W. T. Skye Garcia

Tempo di marcia

Solace

A Mexican Serenade

Scott Joplin

Arr. by W. T. Skye Garcia

Very slow march time

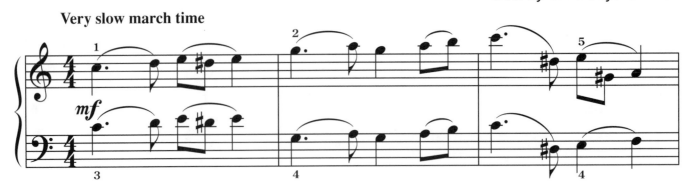

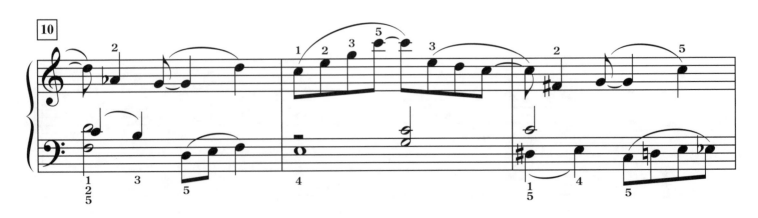

The Augustan Club

Waltzes

Scott Joplin
Arr. by W. T. Skye Garcia

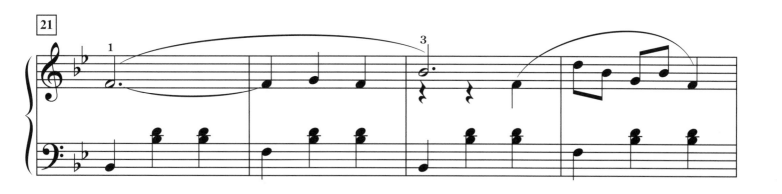

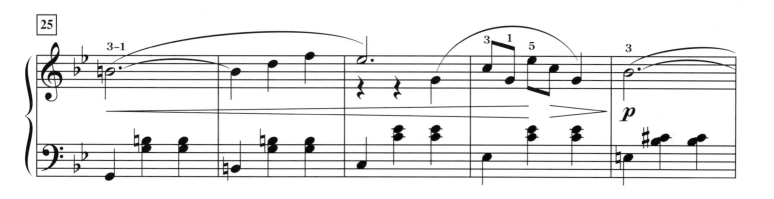

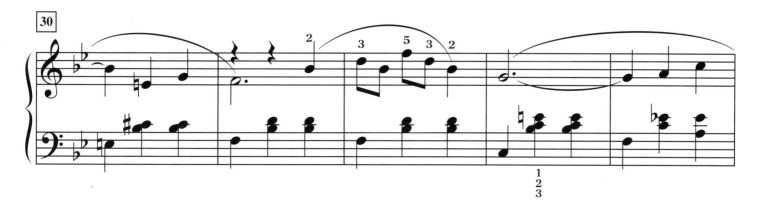

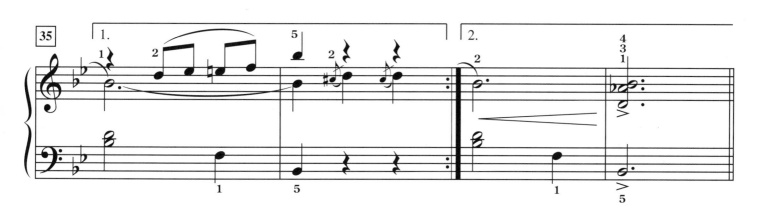

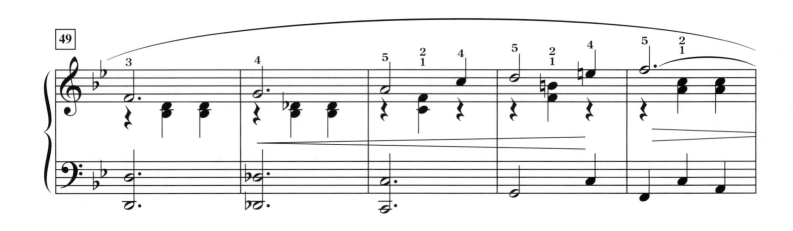

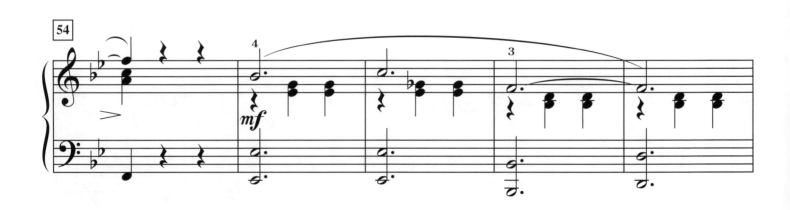

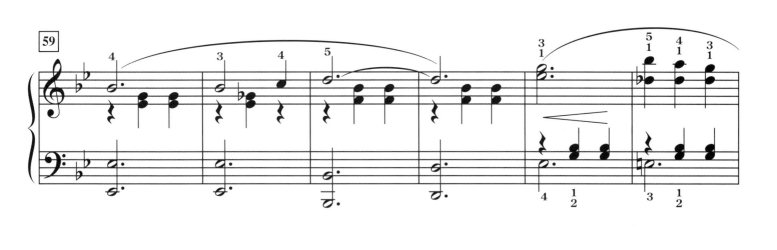

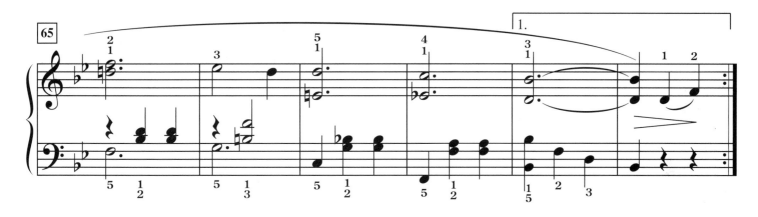

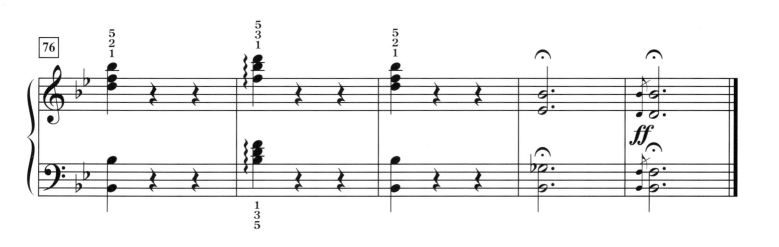

About the Music

Augustan Club, The .... page 28

Written by Scott Joplin, self-proclaimed "King of Ragtime Writers," this piece is not a rag, but a waltz. It was first published in 1901, and, as was the case with many of his compositions (the famous *Maple Leaf Rag* included), it received its name from one of the clubs where Joplin played piano.

Entertainer, The .... page 16

This piece was first published in 1902, a time when Joplin actually referred to himself as *the entertainer.* This rag was at the heart of the ragtime revival of the 1970s—it was used as the theme for the Academy award-winning film, *The Sting.* For Joplin's music, at least, the ragtime revival reached its highpoint in 1976 when the Pulitzer Prize Advisory Board cited Joplin's contribution to American music with a posthumous award. This arrangement contains three of the four original themes.

Maple Leaf Rag .... page 20

Perhaps the most famous of all piano rags, this rag was turned down by at least two different publishers before it was first published by John Stark in 1899. Royalties from its sales provided Joplin with a continuous source of income throughout his life. Joplin himself requested that this piece be played at his funeral. The first two of its four themes are included in this arrangement.

Ragtime Serenade .... page 12

As the title implies, there are really two musical ideas present in this piece. The first is the serenade (measures 5–19)—a musical expression of love and respect for one held dear. It is followed by a spirited rag (measures 20–36) in the relative major—a joyful reminiscence of time gone by. A coda (measures 54–62) resolves the traces of melancholy in the serenade by ending in the parallel major.

Scalawag Rag .... page 8

This ragtime solo features the juxtaposition of chords not normally found together. This creates a harmonic tension that is subsequently resolved. It is an infectiously enthusiastic piece that will engage but not overwhelm the ears of performers, teachers, and audiences alike.

Solace .... page 24

For all of its beauty, warmth and charm, this is perhaps the finest of Joplin's compositions. It was first published in 1909, subtitled *A Mexican Serenade.* The emotional depth of this piece sets it apart as a genuine masterpiece. The B section of the original is not present in this arrangement.

Step Right Up! .... page 2

Eubie Blake (1883–1983) was a composer/pianist from the turn of the 20th century ragtime era. He was known to have written the first rag based on scales. As was the case with many works of this time, it was never written down and sadly, once forgotten, was lost forever. Blake's lost rag provided the inspiration for this piece.

Waltzin' in Ragtime .... page 6

Though this piece is not written in the typical ragtime duple meter, its syncopated melody set against the left hand "oom-pah-pah" accompaniment clearly gives it the "raggedness" that is the signature of all ragtime music.